DEDICATION:

This guide was written by Georgina Bottomley, part of the mrbruf

Georgina Bottomley is an English teacher from Dorset with 15 ye
experience. She is a happily married mother of two. Georgina Bo........y would like
to thank: Andrew Bruff for his valuable time and expert advice when proofreading the
final draft of this book.

I would like to start this eBook by thanking those who have helped and supported
along the way:

- Sam Perkins, who designed the front cover of this eBook.
- Sunny Ratilal, who designed the original front cover which was adapted for
  this edition.

IMPORTANT NOTE:

This guide is not endorsed by, or affiliated with, any exam boards. The writer is
simply an experienced English teacher who is using her skills and expertise to help
students.

Contents:

Introduction to the play

The Curious Incident of the Dog in the Night-Time first appeared in the form of a novel written by Mark Haddon which was published in 2003. Since then it has been adapted for the stage by Simon Stephens and it is this (play) version which is now one of the optional set texts for G.C.S.E. English Literature. Both the novel and the play have been very successful; there have been productions of the play in London, on Broadway and in several other countries.

There are not many works of fiction which revolve around special educational needs and even fewer which use the voice of a narrator who has those additional needs. *The Curious Incident of the Dog in the Night-Time* does just that though. The narrator, Christopher, is on the Autistic Spectrum. In the blurb of the original novel (on which the play is based), Christopher is described as having Aspergers Syndrome, a form of Autism. Nowadays the term Aspergers is rarely used and instead people are just identified as being on the Autistic Spectrum (rather than being neurotypical.) It should be noted however that this condition is never actually named in the novel or the play itself. See the chapter on Context for further information on Autism. Ultimately *Curious Incident* is a story of courage in the face of adversity and an examination of family relationships. Both the novel and play have proved very popular with readers and audiences alike.

Writing your exam answer

When you are writing about this text don't forget to refer to it as a PLAY and concentrate on the effect on an AUDIENCE (rather than a reader). In this way you are showing the examiner that you are well aware of the FORM of the text you are studying.

The new G.C.S.E. exams are "closed book" which means you are unable to take the text you are studying into the exam with you (unlike in previous years, as any older brothers and sisters might tell you!) You must, therefore, learn some quotations. The quotes used in this ebook are carefully chosen and deliberately repeated to help you remember them. Most are "flexible quotes" which could be used for a range of questions on different themes and characters. Specific methods for learning quotes are explored in later chapters.

English lessons prior to G.C.S.E. may well have asked you to pretend you are characters from the texts you have been reading. You might have been asked to complete tasks such as writing diary entries from characters' points of view, or you might have taken part in drama-based activities pretending to be them, or you could have been asked to imagine what could have happened before or after the text. Whilst often enjoyable and certainly an interesting way to engage with the text, this can be problematic at G.C.S.E.

When writing your G.C.S.E. response at NO POINT must you imagine what might have happened before or after the actual events in the text. You must concentrate entirely on HOW the writer has presented the characters and why. It is not an opportunity for being creative (keep that for the creative writing section!) Analysis is the key to your English Literature responses. Focus your response on how the characters have been shown (remember they were deliberately presented that way) and why. What is the effect (or possible effects) on an audience? Don't at any stage be tempted to explore what else the characters might have done etc. Remember they are not real people so don't treat them as if they are. They are the creation of the writer/playwright. Most exam questions will ask you to write about *how* a character is portrayed. The way to address that kind of a question is to explore how Stephens uses **language, structure** and **form** to present key themes and/or characters. All of the main characters and some key themes are explored in greater detail later in this ebook.

Language refers to a writer's deliberate use of specific words or phrases for effect. Remember the playwright also wrote the stage directions so your analysis is not limited to the words the characters actually say. Don't forget to learn the technical terms; do you know what a verb is? An adjective? A noun? An expletive? When writing about this play you should think about the way Christopher speaks aloud in comparison to the way he has written his book. As you'll see he becomes side-tracked easily and uses language to try and maintain order when events around him become confusing or difficult. There is some strong language in both the play and the novel - its use and purpose is explored in some depth later.

Structure refers to the organisation of a text. Initially you might want to consider the order of events and how information is revealed to the audience but you can then go on to think about other structural devices such as repetition. By repeating a word or phrase the writer adds emphasis to it. You could also note the ways in which events have been foreshadowed in the play, examine the use of stage directions and, in the case of *Curious Incident*, analyse how different voices achieve different effects. There is a lengthy chapter in this ebook devoted to the structure of this text.

Form refers to the type of text that you are analysing. *Curious Incident* is a play so it is important that your exam answers show you understand that the text is a play, and as such is different to a novel or poem. Your analysis of stage directions, talking about the AUDIENCE (rather than the reader) and analysing what happens on stage all show that you are well aware of the text's form. Remember, the play version of *Curious Incident* is an adaptation of the novel written by Mark Haddon. The play is written by Simon Stephens. Make sure you refer to the playwright's surname in your answer.

It is important to consider the differences in studying a novel in comparison to a play. Obviously the layout is different with the characters' names listed on the left hand side of the page. There are also some stage directions to take note of which are written in italics. In this play, unlike others you may have studied like *An Inspector Calls* (which starts with a lengthy stage direction which takes up most of the first page), the stage directions in *Curious Incident* are few and far between yet they often reveal crucial information about what we would be seeing on stage. See the chapter on Structure for further analysis of stage directions, along with some key examples.

When we read a novel or a poem it is possible to re-read sections, put it down and come back to it later… a play is different. The audience watching only have one opportunity to understand what they are seeing and to recognise the significance of certain lines or events. Whilst you are reading the playscript, never lose sight of the effect on an audience watching. Their attention must be maintained. At the end of the play, Christopher returns to the stage, thanks the audience for clapping and staying and proceeds to analyse a complicated Maths problem. His interaction with the audience at this point is not always typical of the play form. Usually characters will ignore the audience who are then allowed to be passive viewers of the story. This interaction at the end of *Curious Incident* encourages the audience to be active participants in the story which can certainly be an engaging method for a production to use. Christopher's final line during that interaction states "that is how I got an A grade!!!" reminding the audience of his passion for Maths and how, for him, this is as important to him as many other significant events we have seen during the course of the play.

Context is also important to any text but some exam boards do not assess this for G.C.S.E. so check with your teacher to see if you should include references to this in your answer. The context of this play surrounds the presentation of Christopher as a teenager with Autism and how outsiders or those who are different might be treated by others. See the relevant chapter for further analysis and key quotes.

So, to sum up…. Avoid merely explaining the plot in an exam answer. Don't be imaginative. Instead aim to analyse language, structure, form and context, linking your points to the writer's key themes. Remember to learn some key quotations and don't forget to take care over the accuracy of your spelling, punctuation and grammar!

PLOT SUMMARY:

As the play opens, the audience see a dead dog lying in the middle of the stage with a garden fork sticking out of his side. This dog is Wellington who belonged to Christopher's neighbour Mrs. Shears. Christopher Boone, the fifteen year old protagonist, is on stage along with Mrs. Shears who is questioning what has happened to her dog and telling Christopher to "get away." Siobhan, Christopher's teacher, is also on stage reading from Christopher's book. She provides basic information about Christopher and narrates what happens just as we see the same action unfold on stage, "After twelve and a half minutes a policeman arrived."

Despite being warned to stay out of the issue, Christopher is determined to solve the mystery of the dog's death. Christopher discovers letters from his mother whom he thought was dead and he eventually discovers that his own father lied to him both about the death of his mother and about him having killed Wellington. After losing trust in his father, Christopher flees to London to meet his mother whom his father had told him had died two years prior. Christopher finds the journey to London very challenging but he does eventually find his mother. Ultimately he does return to Swindon to live with his father again but his situation and self-confidence has improved as a result of his adventure. He passes his A level Maths exam at the end of the play, fulfilling another challenge he had set himself.

CONTEXT

As already explained, the action centres around the character of Christopher Boone who would appear to be on the Autistic Spectrum due to his obsessive and repetitive behaviours, his difficulties reading emotions and communicating effectively, and his love of facts and details. This, however, is not explicitly stated in the text. The omission of the title of his condition could lead us to suspect that actually this is not merely a story about Autism. It is a story about the potential isolation of "Outsiders" who might, in some way, be different to the "norm." Even if you haven't met anybody with Autism you might have either felt like an outsider yourself or known someone else to be excluded. There are many reasons why someone might be considered "different." It could be that they are a different race, religion or sexual orientation to a group that they are trying to mix with. People might also feel excluded for having different taste in music or clothes. How tolerant are you and your friends of people you meet who are different to you? There is plenty of scope with this play to consider these issues.

As *Curious Incident* begins, the story may appear to be somewhat of a murder mystery. The audience (and Christopher) are initially presented with the conundrum of who killed Mrs. Shears's dog Wellington. It would be hard to ignore the dead dog on stage which has a garden fork sticking out of it! As soon as the characters start talking, however, it is clear to see that this is more an examination of Christopher and his struggle to fit into a world where people think and express themselves in a way which is different to him and difficult for him to understand. Even the opening exchange between Mrs. Shears and Christopher is fraught. Mark Haddon, the author of the original novel on which the play is based has had experience of working with people with Autism and his understanding of the condition is clear as the play continues and we see Christopher's struggle to fit into a neurotypical world.

You may well have come across people on the Autistic Spectrum at school or in the wider community. People with Aspergers tend to be known as "high functioning" whereas people with classic Autism may be "low functioning," meaning they need a higher level of support to live their everyday lives. People with Autism are all different and the saying goes that "if you have met one person with Autism, you've met one person with Autism." You cannot assume that the person you have met will be like anyone else on that same Autistic Spectrum. That said, there are some common traits of people with Aspergers which fit with the character of Christopher. People with Aspergers tend to be highly intelligent, paying particular attention to details and enjoying order and predictable events. They often dislike changes in routine and can find social situations tricky as they find it harder to read people's facial expressions and non-verbal cues than others who are neurotypical. Some young people with different forms of Autism go to schools which specialise in meeting their specific needs, whereas others do very well in mainstream schools.

The issues with communication are very applicable to the world in which we all live. Thanks to the advancements in technology we are able to communicate more frequently with one another but primarily this might be via a computer or mobile phone screen as social media sites continue to thrive and text messages are sent far more often than phone calls or visits to that person are ever made. Computer games also encourage live communication but again all via the safety of the screen. Christopher acknowledges the protection in these forms of communication during the play when he imagines being in Space, "I would have to talk to other people from Mission Control, but we would do that through a radio link-up and a TV monitor so it wouldn't be like real people who are strangers but it would be like playing a computer game." His language here clearly demonstrates a desire for adventure but he also recognises his difficulties with face-to-face communication.

Some may argue that our skills of verbal and non-verbal communication are suffering as a result of our increased time spent communicating via digital means. Even those without Autism may start to find eye contact more challenging and may worry about not knowing what to say in response during a conversation if we don't have the extra time to think that text or other forms of messaging allow us. The play enables these issues to be explored in depth.

STRUCTURE:

The structure of the text is the way in which it is organised. You must consider the structure of the play in any exam answer. Initially you might want to consider the order of events and how information is revealed to the audience but you can then go on to think about other structural devices such as repetition. By repeating a word or phrase the writer adds emphasis to it. You could also think about the way events have been foreshadowed in the play, the use of stage directions and, in the case of *Curious Incident*, how different voices achieve different effects. Unlike in most plays, there are no regular act and scene changes in *Curious Incident*. In this play the scenes run into one another without interruption. Despite this the playwright does manage to include several different places and times within the story. The audience are required to be active participants and piece everything together as they watch the play.

So let's begin by thinking about when the main events happen in *Curious Incident*… does the story begin at the beginning and end at the end? The answer to this question is, of course, no!

Chronology

The order and use of time is known as the "chronology" of the play. *Curious Incident* is written in two parts (rather than the usual acts and scenes we so often see in playscripts) and has a non-linear structure; events are revealed in a different order to which they occurred. For example, we find out who killed Wellington the dog after it happened and we find out that Christopher's mother Judy went to live in London with Mr Shears part way through the play whereas we initially believe the same as Christopher, that she had died. There are also flashbacks such as when Christopher explains how his father told him that his mother had been admitted to hospital (when, in fact, she had left to go to London with Mr. Shears). Remember, none of these structural features occur by accident. The non-linear nature of the text could well reflect the way Christopher's mind works. The audience often see him struggle to maintain a logical approach to the difficulties he encounters. Just as his mind easily wanders off track, so we the audience also have to work at piecing the parts of the mysteries together ourselves.

Curious Incident has a fairly dramatic opening as the first scene we see contains a dead dog with a pitchfork sticking out of it, followed by Mrs. Shears asking Christopher, "What in Christ's name have you done to my dog?" This whodunit/murder mystery is set up as a driving force for the action but the text is more an exploration of Christopher's character and his ability to overcome the difficulties he has with communication and with his family situation, rather than the focus being on who actually killed Wellington the dog. This opening scene does effectively grab the attention of an audience however as they too begin by wondering who could be cruel enough to kill an innocent animal using a pitchfork. Violence is a theme which is further explored as the play progresses.

Journeys

Just as Christopher embarks on a challenging physical journey to London, so he also goes on a psychological journey. It can appear as if Christopher is struggling with the physical aspects of the journey, but the play's focus is also on his ability to accept that his parents are fallible; his father lied to him and his mother had an affair. Christopher must battle with his emotions as much as his physical reactions to the environment around him. By the end of the play there is still work to be done by Christopher and his family but the future is looking more positive for those relationships. Remember in an exam to focus on what is revealed in the play and how it is left. It is fine to say that unanswered questions remain for the audience but you should avoid speculating on what might happen next. Focus instead on why the playwright might have chosen to leave the audience with those questions…

If you are analysing an extract from the play, consider whereabouts in the play that scene occurs. Is it the opening? (See the end of this ebook for a sample essay on the first two pages of the playscript). Is it the end of the play? Is it setting up any future events? Examiners will choose an extract which is of importance in the play. Re-reading the play several times (and seeing it on stage if possible) will help you to recognise quickly when and where that scene occurs. You must get to know the plot thoroughly. See "Ways of remembering the plot" for revision techniques which focus on this skill. Do not rely on reading short summaries as your revision, you need to be able to recognise where extracts are from so you need to be very familiar with the play.

Voices

Again in the early part of the play we hear Christopher's inner thoughts and feelings courtesy of Siobhan (his teacher) who reads aloud from his book. We hear Siobhan read from the book in the opening scene so we are seeing the action on stage at the same time as hearing about it from Christopher' book. This book is written in the style of a diary and it is an effective structural device which allows us an insight into Christopher's mind at times when he might find it difficult to communicate (such as when he is being blamed for the death of the dog). In Part Two we learn that Christopher's book has been turned into a play by his school so it can be thought of as a "play within a play."

Other voices are used at different times in the play in addition to the main characters which would be seen on stage. They are used in the play to narrate what we are seeing such as Voices 1-6 that reveal the contents of Christopher's pockets as he empties them for the policeman after his arrest. This is somewhat unusual but does remind the audience of Christopher's love of details.

Freytag's Pyramid

Freytag's Pyramid is a theory of dramatic structure. Freytag was a German novelist who examined the plots of stories and discovered a common structure (see diagram).

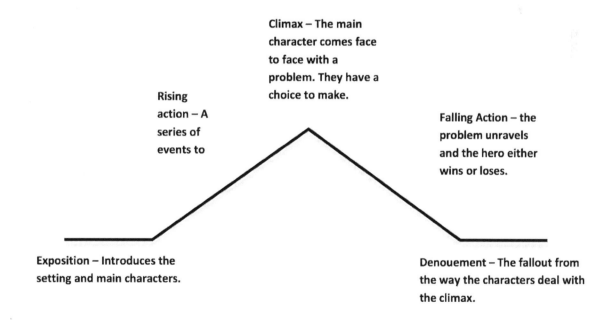

Climax – The main character comes face to face with a problem. They have a choice to make.

Rising action – A series of events to

Falling Action – the problem unravels and the hero either wins or loses.

Exposition – Introduces the setting and main characters.

Denouement – The fallout from the way the characters deal with the climax.

Exposition is the setting of the scene in the first place. The tension rises and builds towards a main event, otherwise known as the "climax" of the story before the suspense gradually reduces as we get to denouement, the ending where any remaining issues are resolved and questions are answered.

In *Curious Incident*, the Exposition sets the scene: we are in Swindon with Christopher having discovered the dead body of his neighbour Mrs. Shears's dog. The Rising Action is when, as he is investigating the murder of Wellington the dog, Christopher discovers the letters written to him from his mother who his father had told him had died. The climax of the story occurs when, after a difficult journey, Christopher arrives in London to confront his mother. The Falling Action is the time that Christopher spends with his mother in London whilst he begins to repair the relationship with his father. By the end of the play the mystery of who killed the dog has been solved, but so has the mystery of what had happened to his mother. The play ends with hope for the future that the family relationships will have been repaired (the denouement).

Stage Directions

Whether analysing an extract or a theme or character in the play, consider the playwright's use of stage directions. There are very few stage directions in *Curious Incident*. The playwright leaves it to the characters to tell the story with little interference. Despite being sparse, the stage directions do show how Christopher or other characters use non-verbal communication. Christopher can rely on non-verbal communication to express himself or, in this part of the play, to block out the situation he is finding challenging to deal with (being falsely accused of the murder of Mrs. Shears's dog). "Christopher puts his hands over his ears. He closes his eyes… He starts groaning." Like Mrs. Shears, the stress of the situation has caused Christopher's linguistic abilities to crumble. He resorts to blocking his senses. Christopher relies on physical methods of communication at other points in the play too such as when he gets into a fight with his father, "Ed shakes Christopher hard… Christopher punches Ed repeatedly in the face." Non-verbal communication is also used between Christopher and his parents as due to his dislike of physical touch, they spread their fingers and touch those together instead, rather than giving hugs which might be the preferred means of comfort from other parents to their children. Make sure you look out for the stage directions and learn some quotes from them as you are then also showing an awareness of the form of the text (it's a play!).

Sentence length and Punctuation

The length of the sentences and the use of punctuation can reveal more about the way in which a character is feeling when those lines are delivered. An example would be when Judy refers to Ed as "Bastard." The short sentences sum up her thoughts about him as she finds out Ed had told their son that she'd died, rather than telling the truth (that she had had an affair with Mr. Shears and gone to live with him in London). On stage, the use of these short sentences with expletives could actually be used for comic effect depending on how those lines are delivered. If this is the case it could offer a moment of light relief and provide a contrast to the difficult situation Christopher finds himself in in London.

Look out for exclamation marks, use of ellipsis etc. to show whether lines are delivered with vigour and enthusiasm or whether the character is struggling to find the right words (such as when Ed repeatedly uses ellipses when trying to explain to Christopher how he needs to regain his trust near the end of the play). Repetition is another technique which is used to add emphasis to the words being used. There are many examples of repetition being used throughout "Curious Incident" including when, near the end of the play, Ed requests a talk with Christopher, his son initially repeats the word "No" seven times to emphasise his lack of desire to enter into a conversation with his father at that time.

Don't forget to include the word "structure" in your exam answer. Revise the different techniques thoroughly and if necessary write down key words such as repetition, flashbacks, voices etc. as soon as you get into the exam. That way you won't have to remember them, they'll be there on your page as a prompt to include them in your answer.

CHARACTER ANALYSIS: CHRISTOPHER BOONE – protagonist, narrator

Christopher is the narrator of the novel. He is a 15 year old boy who has Aspergers Syndrome, a form of Autism (see the chapter on Context for more information on Autism and the Autistic Spectrum). Christopher hates novels because they are fictional but ironically here he is, a fictional character who has been writing a fictional novel whilst appearing in a fictional play! This irony and use of paradox is no doubt entertaining for an audience.

Due to his condition, Christopher has very set rules about what he (and others) are allowed to do. He also likes facts and subjects such as Maths and Science which have right and wrong answers. English is a subject where it is acceptable to read things in different ways and offer different interpretations of meaning depending on what the reader brings to the table. For example, one teacher might read a student's piece of creative writing and think it is brilliant and original whereas another teacher may have come across a similar storyline elsewhere, maybe in a TV show or another text and so is likely to be less impressed than the first. Open ended texts some readers find intriguing and enjoyable to read as they must continue to consider the possibilities whereas other readers might find this structure frustrating and would prefer a definitive ending. Which do you prefer? Subjects which are more black and white, right and wrong, or those where there are grey areas and your opinions are welcome? Your thoughts can then be applied to whether or not you can relate to the character of Christopher and his love of the truth and facts.

The use of a first person narrator is always interesting. The story is mainly told from Christopher's point of view, especially since we hear his thoughts and feelings through his book as well as the actual lines he says on stage. It is easy to assume that because a character is talking that they are giving an honest and fair appraisal of the situation. But is that really true? Do people always speak the truth? There is a potential for that narrator's comments to be unreliable, even in the case of

Christopher who says he always speaks the truth. Is he being honest when he says that? John Mullan (a senior lecturer in English at University College, London), in his article entitled "Through Innocent Eyes" which appeared in *The Guardian* newspaper, explains how Christopher is more of an inadequate narrator, rather than just being unreliable. His lack of ability to communicate effectively and his struggle to read the emotions and feelings of others means that we possibly don't always hear the whole story from Christopher. He appears trustworthy and explains that he always tells the truth but how much has Christopher missed whilst, for example, being curled into a ball or screaming?

Christopher is academically bright but really struggles in social situations and when the outcome of an encounter or situation is unpredictable. He can react in quite a physical way. When Mrs Shears tells him to get away from her dead dog in the opening of the play the stage directions tell us Christopher closes his eyes, puts his hands over his ears and groans. The playwright makes us aware from the very beginning that this is a character who reacts in an unusual way to stress. Christopher also groans whilst being questioned by the police officer. The repetition of the groaning adds emphasis to the way in which Christopher loses his language and is only able to make noises at these tricky times. He does not have the communication skills of most teenagers who are not on the Autistic Spectrum and tends to be more physical and communicate non-verbally. He even hits a policeman who tries to lift him up. The playwright gives us many reasons to find Christopher difficult to relate to at the start of the play. This structure allows the audience to truly appreciate how much progress Christopher makes during the course of the play.

Early in the play during a conversation with his father about why he would like to be an astronaut Christopher reveals more about himself. We learn that Christopher, like many others with Autism, likes his own company and finds comfort in enclosed areas, "I really like little spaces so long as there is no one else in them with me." It is also apparent that he finds face-to-face interactions challenging (again as do many others on the Autistic Spectrum), "I would have to talk to other people from Mission Control, but we would do that through a radio link-up and a TV monitor so it wouldn't be like real people who are strangers but it would be like playing a computer game." By placing these comments early in the play the playwright makes it clear that Christopher finds social interaction difficult. Communication is a key theme in the play and something that most of us take for granted. This theme is explored in greater depth later in this ebook.

Individuals with Autism often find it difficult to read facial expressions and emotions in others so may prefer to communicate in other ways such as via text message or the internet. Unlike some Autistic people though, Christopher does seem able to imagine situations such pretending what it would be like to be in space whereas others on the same spectrum can find that hard. Christopher does recognise that he is different to other people but he can't really understand why anyone would want to interact socially. Siobhan reads from his book which sounds very much like a diary and sums up his thoughts, "I find people confusing." He is happy to retreat into his own world and imagination. Despite this though he can find it difficult to put himself in someone else's shoes and so is quite distant from other people including his own father whom he lives with.

The interactions between Christopher and his father demonstrate his difficulties with social relationships. There is a moment when his father offers a seemingly very sincere apology to his son after their fight but whilst they do touch hands, Christopher is thinking about where his book is. The structure of these comments alongside the non-verbal communication seems to suggest the two characters might look like they're reconnecting but actually Christopher's mind is wandering. See the chapter on Ed Boone for further analysis of this relationship.

Christopher's conversations with his teacher Siobhan provide an interesting contrast to those we see between Christopher and his father. With her he explores his thoughts about the possible killer of Wellington, he talks about his mother and sometimes even talks to her in his mind. He can also chat about his interests such as Maths, maybe because Siobhan doesn't put any pressure on him, "If you say you don't want to do it no one is going to be angry with you.". He remembers her advice when sitting his Maths A level. It is as if Siobhan is taking the role of the main female influence in Christopher's life in the absence of his mother. However, it is important to remember that despite Christopher wanting to go and live with her at the end of the play she refuses, giving the clear reason, "it's because I'm not your mother." Her position as a support remains but she never becomes an actual replacement for Christopher's mother. See the chapter on Siobhan for further analysis of her role in the play.

Christopher is happier being alone and engaging in activities such as reading and problem solving by himself. His book (read by Siobhan) reveals his love of facts and figures, "I know all the countries of the world… and every prime number up to 7507." Comments such as these could alienate Christopher as a character. An audience may not be able to identify with his passion for facts and figures but by adding these comments near the start of the play it again sets up a key theme which is revisited throughout the text, that of truth. See the chapter on truth and lies for a detailed analysis of this theme. It is also possible that an audience may not be able to relate to Christopher too easily and therefore may not feel too much sympathy for him here at the start of the play but this may well change as we see that actually Christopher can overcome some of the challenges presented to him; he can show perseverance and determination when needed as he successfully makes the trip to London to see his mother.

There are many different possible aspects to Christopher's condition; Autistic people can find different aspects of everyday life challenging. As the play progresses, more is revealed about how Christopher sees the world and how his thinking can be somewhat narrowed by his condition. We find out he doesn't like the colours yellow or brown, "it's red food colouring because I don't eat yellow food." This may seem unreasonable to an audience. He also doesn't like to be touched, even by members of his own family. He can become angry when he feels a situation is out of his control. Again at this stage of the play an audience may find Christopher difficult to relate to.

Also in the opening of the play we find out that Christopher has an excellent memory and loves Science and Maths, probably because they are quite black and white, right and wrong. He genuinely enjoys solving Maths equations so when faced with the mystery of who killed his neighbour's dog, Wellington, he sees it as another problem he can solve. Christopher does not like metaphors because they are confusing to him; he sees them as a form of lie, "because a pig is not like a day and people do not have skeletons in their cupboards." He does occasionally use similes though such as, "The rain looks like white sparks." This might be because the comparison is weaker than a metaphor which says something IS something which it isn't really. Maybe Christopher does have some ability to draw these kinds of comparisons and understand some figures of speech.

Like any teenager, Christopher is striving for independence but since he struggles with unfamiliar situations he is somewhat torn between wanting to operate alone and actually being able to do so practically. He argues with his father and goes alone to London, even though the journey is extremely arduous for him. He even wets himself whilst on the train, another physical reaction in a time of stress. The policeman he encounters on the journey is less than sympathetic. As Christopher is groaning whilst being questioned the policeman says, "Young man… stop making that noise…." He is then sarcastic when Christopher fails to stop, "Marvellous." We have to ask, might that also be the reaction of lots of audience members too if they see someone unable to cope in a situation that most manage every day without thinking about it? Or is this actually the point at which we can start to sympathise with Christopher as despite finding the journey extremely challenging and stressful he is still determined to complete it and find his mother in London. Your opinion is very valid as long as you can back it up with textual references and clear analysis.

When he arrives in London we see Christopher initially struggling to connect with his mother. She tries to give him a hug then remembers he doesn't like to be touched and instead makes contact with people he knows as trusts (such as his parents) by spreading his fingers. In this way the audience are shown how he does find methods to communicate and does have patience and understanding when seeing his mother years after thinking she had died. It might have been easy for him to be angry or dismissive after his parents had lied to him but instead Christopher sees the need to reconnect with his mother after all. The structure of the play allows the audience to see the growth in Christopher as more of his admirable qualities emerge.

Before leaving, Christopher explained how he was now afraid of his father, "Father had murdered Wellington. That meant he could murder me." The word "murder" suggests a planned attack designed to deliberately kill. The use of alliteration in "murder me" is memorable. Instead of being able to go to his parents in times of difficulty and stress, Christopher is having to run away. He repeats "I had to get out of the house" five times. This use of repetition by the playwright could show Christopher's inability to get past that one thought in his mind. It's all he can think about, so the line is repeated until he can move on. The book being read shows what is happening in Christopher's mind that he might not always be able to express verbally. When he next sees his father in London, Christopher points a Swiss Army knife at him, again communicating his thoughts and feelings in a non-verbal way but one which is becoming increasingly easier for an audience to understand as they get used to his methods of communication. The appearance of a knife would be particularly dramatic on stage. Arguably no words are even needed at this point! The tensions between Christopher and his father are further explored in another chapter in this ebook as it is a key theme in the play.

By the end of the play Christopher's self-esteem has improved. Despite his struggle, he did manage to travel to London and did uncover the truth… not only that his own father killed Wellington the dog but that his mother is alive and well in London. His relationships with his parents have evolved and show positivity in regard to the future. The playwright shows the audience that people such as Christopher, with differences or disabilities can still achieve their aims.

Check your understanding: Christopher Boone

1. What form of Autism does Christopher have?

2. Why does Christopher prefer subjects like Maths and Science over English?

3. How does Christopher react when Mrs. Shears tells him to get away from her dead dog?

4. Why might some people with Autism find it easier to communicate with other people over the internet or via text message?

5. How does the communication and connection Christopher has with Siobhan differ to that which he has with his father?

6. Who does Christopher want to live with at the end of the play?

7. Which two colours does Christopher dislike?

8. Why doesn't Christopher like metaphors?

9. Why does Christopher become afraid of his father?

10. How is Christopher's self-esteem by the end of the play?

CHARACTER ANALYSIS: ED BOONE (Christopher's father)

Ed Boone is Christopher's father. He is separated from Christopher's mother and now takes sole care of Christopher. There are some similarities between Ed Boone and his son. Firstly, he also sometimes struggles with communication and, just like Christopher, can react in quite an angry manner as shown by his use of expletives, "Don't give me that bollocks you little shit." Both can also react in physical ways when pushed, as the stage directions explain, "Ed shakes Christopher hard... Christopher punches Ed repeatedly in the face." Ed appears genuinely sorry for having reacted in this way after they have both calmed down. He (unlike Christopher as previously explained) genuinely seems to want to reconnect with his son at this moment whereas Christopher is more focused on where his book is. See the chapter on family tensions for further analysis of this quote and others which relate to that theme.

Ed can be further criticised for having lied to his son. He told Christopher that his wife, Christopher's mother, had died when actually she had left him and had an affair. He also doesn't initially confess to having killed Wellington the dog. When Christopher finds out what really happened this creates distance and mistrust between him and his father. Christopher runs away to London to find his mother as a result of his father's lies. The structure used here – the gradual revelation of the details increase the tension as we wonder what other lies Ed has been hiding. This structure can lead the audience to have little sympathy for Mr. Boone due to these flaws but there are positive aspects to his character which are also worthy of analysis. These positive aspects run alongside the negatives; we don't see the flaws at the start replaced by the praiseworthy aspects of his character. In this way he presents as a believable character who can be praised and criticised at the same time.

 Ed doesn't appear to have that many friends so his son seems to be one of his main companions. This is confirmed by the playwright's use of language as Ed even refers to his son as "mate" at times. He takes good care of Christopher and is very understanding of his specific needs and routines. He prepares food which Christopher will eat, an example being when Christopher requests the unusual combination of baked beans and broccoli for dinner, "I think that can be very easily arranged." Despite the obvious difficulties, Ed appears consistently anxious to protect his son. Even Judy, his ex-wife, is complimentary about him in one of the letters she has written to Christopher. In comparison to herself she says, "Your father is a much more patient person." Whilst possibly not used deliberately, the alliterative "patient person" makes this quote quite memorable.

Overall, Ed is presented as a character who is trapped, firstly by the limitations of where he can take his son and avoid situations Christopher would find stressful, and secondly by his lies. He not only lied about his killing of Wellington and the fact his wife is still alive (and he had been hiding her letter to Christopher), but also about his own affair with Mrs. Shears.

Despite the difficulties between Ed and Christopher, by the end of the play the damage seems to have been somewhat repaired and the relationship between father and son seems back on track. Ed tells his son he's proud of him. There are further reminders from Ed about how challenging it has been for him to be close to his son, particularly due to the communication difficulties between them, "You being in the house but refusing to talk to me." Christopher "refusing to talk" underlines how he finds communication, particularly verbal communication, difficult.

At the end of the play Ed is determined to improve things and to get Christopher to trust him again. He is initially rejected by his son when he says he'd like to talk to him; his request is merely met by Christopher repeating the word "No..." Again the playwright uses repetition to add emphasis. He perseveres though and Ed explains his main aim for the future, "And I... I have to show you that you can trust me... and it will be difficult at first because... because it's a difficult project." During the speech the sentences are broken and an ellipsis is used repeatedly to show how Ed is having to pause and think through exactly what to say to his son to repair the damaged relationship. It would seem he recognises his lies as wrongdoings and is determined to rebuild a positive relationship with his son as they return to Swindon together.

Check your understanding: Ed Boone

1. What is Ed's relationship status at the start of the play?

2. What are the similarities between Ed and his son?

3. Give an example of Ed's use of expletives when he's talking to Christopher...

4. What lies do we find out Ed has been telling Christopher?

5. What does Ed call his son which suggests he sometimes sees him as a friend?

6. How does Judy describe Ed in comparison to herself?

7. Who has Ed been having an affair with?

8. How has the situation between Ed and Christopher improved by the end of the play?

9. What does the writer's repeated use of ellipses during Ed's speech near the end of the play reveal about Ed's state of mind at this time?

10. What is Ed determined to do by the end of the play?

CHARACTER ANALYSIS: JUDY BOONE (Christopher's mother)

Judy Boone is Christopher's mother. At the beginning of the play Christopher believes his mother is dead as that is what his father told him after Judy left him. We, the audience, naturally believe this too as no alternative is suggested at this point. The discovery of the letters Judy has written to Christopher is a pivotal moment in the play. We can have sympathy for Christopher's extreme reaction to the revelation as we too are shocked at the lies his father Ed has told him.

Christopher remembers his mother as someone who used to get cross with him and seemed unable to handle the specifics of his condition. He is told by Mrs. Alexander that his mother had had an affair with Mr. Shears, "I mean they were very good friends. Very, very good friends." The repetition of "very" makes it clear to the audience that this was much more than a friendship which had been struck up between the two characters. Judy is actually now living with Mr. Shears in London.

During the course of the play Christopher discovers his mother's letters to him and it is these that explain the truth about what happened between her and Christopher's father and how difficult she found it dealing with Christopher's, at times, extreme behaviour. She even says that she believed herself to be "not a very good mother". She seems to think that Christopher was better off living with his father as she thought his behaviour was better with his Dad. She explains how Ed is a "more patient person" and how Christopher was "much calmer" when with his dad. The alliteration in "patient person" makes this phrase memorable and emphasises the contrast between Christopher's two parents. After a difficult day trying to deal with Christopher's challenging behaviour in town Judy explains how she came home and "cried and cried and cried." The repetition here emphasises her strength of feeling and emotion about their living situation at the time.

Ed and Christopher have moments of violence, "Ed shakes Christopher hard... Christopher punches Ed repeatedly in the face" but Judy is also capable of lashing out in a physical way and admits to hitting her husband when he told her to pull herself together. She describes, again via her letters how she "decided it would be better for all of us if I went." Her use of language here, "better for all of us" suggests that she isn't just thinking about herself and her own desire to be with Mr. Shears, but also about what might enable Christopher and Ed to be happy too. In this way an audience may go beyond Judy's initial presentation as a character who ran off and had an affair to someone who was struggling to communicate with her son and who actually wanted the best for her family.

After initially trying to hug Christopher when she sees him for the first time in London, Judy quickly remembers and spreads her fingers and touches his hands that way. Both Christopher's parents have a way of calming and communicating with him though and that is through the touch of their fingers to his. This non-verbal communication takes the place of verbal communication that parents might more commonly use to calm their children. It would be very challenging for Judy as Christopher's mother, not to be able to hug and kiss him to comfort him as most other mothers might with their own children. It is arguably easier to see this as an expression of love on stage as the audience watch their fingers slowly meet.

When Christopher and his mother eventually do begin to reconnect she still seems to fear his behaviour to some extent. Happily she is able to move beyond these fears and express her love for her son. Judy is very pleased to see him, has never forgotten about him and has written him many letters since she last saw him. Soon after they are reunited her language demonstrates her affection as she calls him "love" and "sweetheart". On finding out that Ed had lied to Christopher by saying she had died again we see her strength of feeling through her use of language and repetition, "Bastard. The Bastard." The short sentences sum up how she feels about Ed at that moment. The use of capital letters is as if she has given him a derogatory title.

Whereas Ed, Christopher's father, is very supportive of his academic interests such as his passion for Maths and Science, his mother is less keen to allow him to pursue these further. She postpones him sitting his Maths A level for a year but when this is met by Christopher screaming non-stop she does relent and rearrange it. This occurs near the end of the play and seems to symbolise a reconciliation between the family members. The audience are left with the message that it is possible for families to move beyond their difficulties and continue to build a life together in the future.

Check your understanding: Judy Boone

1. What does Christopher believe has happened to his mother at the start of

the play?

2. At which point in the play does Christopher realise that his father has been lying to him about his mother?

3. How does Christopher remember his mother when he thinks about their past relationship?

4. Which character told Christopher that his mother had been having an affair with Mr. Spears?

5. Where is Judy actually living and who with?

6. What does Judy think of her own parenting skills?

7. When she first sees Christopher again, how does Judy do try to greet him (which Christopher doesn't appreciate?)

8. What does she do next to greet him more successfully?

9. What does Judy call her son which shows she really does care for him?

10. What does Judy call Ed when he finds out he has been lying to Christopher and saying she'd died?

CHARACTER ANALYSIS: SIOBHAN (Christopher's teacher, 27 years old, also used as a narrator)

The use of Siobhan in the play is very interesting. In a novel (as opposed to a play) it can be easy to hear the thoughts of characters within the text depending on how it has been written. Of course, if a novel is written solely in the first or third person that is limiting in itself as we then only hear the voice of the narrator or the voice of the one character. A play allows for several voices but when you see those characters on stage the challenge changes to one where it is difficult to present their innermost thoughts without having frequent monologues.

The original novel is written in the first person but in the play Siobhan is seen reading out extracts from the book Christopher has written (the book that has become the play). The first thing she does on stage at the very beginning of the play is to open Christopher's book and read from it, telling the story of when he found Wellington with a fork sticking out of his side in Mrs. Shears's garden. It is as if Siobhan is narrating what we're seeing on stage at this time as whilst she is reading we are watching Mrs Shears talk to Christopher as they stand over her dead dog. The use of Siobhan reading out Christopher's book is a structural device which is further explored in the chapter entitled Structure. Other voices are used in the play to narrate what we are seeing such as Voices 1-6 that reveal the contents of Christopher's pockets as he empties them for the policeman after his arrest.

However, to further complicate the structure and the use of narrative voice, Siobhan also acts and speaks as Christopher's teacher, sometimes whilst she comments on what she is reading aloud from his book, "Siobhan says that if you raise one eyebrow it can mean lots of different things. It can mean 'I want to do sex with you.' I never said that." This grammatically incorrect sentence shows that Christopher doesn't actually understand the significance of his words here. He seems naive, possibly due to his lack of desire for much communication with other people. It can also be used as a moment of light relief and make the audience laugh. In this quote it is Siobhan that says, "I never said that," whereas the rest is from Christopher's book which she is reading out. Think about whether this complication is the playwright's clever use of voices or whether this could be considered confusing. Arguably if the play is seen on stage Siobhan's movement and body language would make it far easier to understand who is talking at any given time.

Later in the play Siobhan reads from the letters that Judy, Christopher's mother, sent. Siobhan almost acts like a mother figure to Christopher at times during the play when his actual mother isn't present. Due to the fractured relationships between Christopher and his parents, Siobhan is able to offer support and understanding to Christopher. She recognises how his achievements in Maths allow him to gain some self-confidence and so (in contrast to his mother) is supportive of him sitting his Maths A level but without putting unnecessary pressure on him, "If you say you don't want to do it no one is going to be angry with you." It is important to remember that despite Christopher wanting to go and live with her at the end of the play she refuses giving the clear reason, "it's because I'm not your mother." Her position as a support remains but she never becomes an actual replacement for Christopher's mother.

Interestingly it is only really worthwhile to analyse Siobhan in terms of her relationship with Christopher. Her interactions with him (including her reading from his book) drive her appearances on stage. We, the audience, know very little about her background or life beyond her time with Christopher. In this way she can be seen as a dramatic device which helps us to further understand the character of Christopher.

Check your understanding: Siobhan

1. Who is Siobhan and how does she know Christopher?

2. How old is Siobhan?

3. How does Siobhan act as a narrator as well as a character in her own right?

4. Which other texts does Siobhan read from during the play?

5. Give an example of other voices used in the play…

6. How does Siobhan act as a mother figure to Christopher?

7. Why does Siobhan adopt the role of a mother figure to Christopher?

8. Siobhan supports Christopher's decision to sit his Maths A level but what does she say to him to try and avoid putting unnecessary pressure on him?

9. Why doesn't Siobhan let Christopher go and live with her at the end of the play?

10. How much do we know about Siobhan's own life or background beyond her relationship and support for Christopher?

CHARACTER ANALYSES: The Minor Characters

Mrs. Alexander is an elderly neighbour of Christopher's. She is friendly towards Christopher and treats him with kindness, showing that not everyone will see Christopher as someone to be mocked and laughed at. Her most important moment is when she reveals that Christopher's mother has had an affair with Mr. Shears.

Mr Roger Shears is seen living in London with Christopher's mother Judy. He was previously married to Mrs. Shears whose dog has died at the beginning of the play. When Christopher arrives at their house in London he doesn't seem keen for him to stay, "this flat is hardly big enough for two people." He is quickly overruled by Judy,

Christopher's mother though, showing she seems to have the most control in the relationship.

Mrs. Shears and Christopher's father Ed Boone have had a relationship but the situation turned sour and led to Ed killing the dog which is discovered dead at the beginning of the play. She is still living in Swindon and has the opening line accusing Christopher of killing her dog, "What in Christ's name have you done to my dog?" She is rude to Judy when she comes back with Christopher, "You've got a bloody nerve." This metaphor and the use of the expletive "bloody" shows how she is still angry about Judy having had an affair with her husband.

The policemen Christopher meets are not nearly as understanding or patient as an audience might expect them to be, "If you try any of that monkey-business again, you little shit, I am going to seriously lose my rag." This links with the theme of the fallibility of adults. The use of the expletives and the metaphor "I am going to seriously lose my rag" shows policemen struggle to understand Christopher and give him the time and respect he needs to enable effective communication to take place between them. Christopher finds it difficult to understand metaphors and dislikes them so this also sets up conflict between the two characters.

Wellington is the dog that Christopher discovers dead at the beginning of the play. He belonged to Mrs. Shears, Christopher's neighbour and it is his death that drives the element of mystery and "whodunit" in the plot.

Toby the rat belongs to Christopher and is a source of companionship for him; Christopher sees him as a member of the family. Christopher takes him to London and finds comfort in his presence.

There are additional voices and very minor characters such as "Man with Socks" and other voices who may have a few lines. Do not worry about learning all of these very minor characters as most are just there to drive the narrative along.

REMEMBER! No matter which character you are analysing, remember to focus on details from the text, at no point should you imagine them to be real people. Make sure you consider WHY the playwright has presented them in that way, concentrate on the language they use and the actions they take (remember to study the stage directions!)

Check your understanding: Minor Characters

1. Who is Mrs. Alexander?

2. How does Mrs. Alexander treat Christopher?

3. What important information does Mrs. Alexander reveal to Christopher?

4. Where is Mr. Spears now?

5. Who owns the dog which has died at the start of the play?

6. How does Mr. Shears react when Christopher arrives at their London flat?

7. Why did Ed kill Wellington the dog?

8. Who did Mrs. Shears first blame for he death of her dog?

9. How do the policemen Christopher meets treat him?

10. What other animal (belonging to Christopher) do we meet during the play?

THEMES

Attitudes to disability (or difference): awareness and acceptance

Whilst the opening scene suggests the play might primarily be about discovering who killed Wellington the dog, it actually can be seen as an exploration of how outsiders, in this case Christopher who has Autism, struggle to relate to others and strive to function effectively in the modern world.

In an interview Mark Haddon explains that the original novel (on which the play is based) is not just about Autism as a disability but about how people are different to one another. Audience members are prompted to question their own attitudes to difference, abilities and disabilities.

Christopher looks physically the same as any other child but he really struggles both mentally and physically when presented with challenging situations. His verbal language and body language reflect this. Remember to comment on the use of stage directions in any exam answer. Stephens highlights Christopher's disability through the stage directions such as when he curls himself into a ball in an animalistic way to avoid a situation or when he repeats words or phrases such as his repetition of the word "No." His disability seriously affects his ability to communicate and so he sometimes relies on non-verbal communication to express his thoughts and feelings.

In the play we see Christopher lash out, sometimes in a violent way, for example when he hits his father, "Christopher punches Ed repeatedly in the face" and he strikes the policeman who grabbed him by the arms. He doesn't react in the way a neurotypical teenager would. He doesn't have the language skills or the understanding of others' emotions to be able to cope with confrontations so in some ways he presents more like a toddler. Very young children tend to lash out, sit down on the floor in protest or scream when they don't know how to verbally express what they are feeling.

When analysing this theme it is essential to consider how others react in response to Christopher. Mrs. Shears at the start of the play assumes Christopher has killed her dog, "What in Christ's name have you done to my dog?" This assumption could just be based on him standing in her garden over the dead dog or it could be she is aware of his potential for violent outbursts. Either way, she gives him little chance to explain and is clearly intolerant to his disability. The question engages an audience who may also assume that Christopher was responsible for the dog's death, either due to his inability to explain himself or because of Mrs. Shears's wording which implies he was to blame, "What in Christ's name have YOU done..." Upon realising that Christopher actually had nothing to do with the death of the dog it is up to an audience to reflect on whether or not they had jumped to the incorrect conclusion too. Could Christopher's unusual behaviour and lack of verbal communication lead people to think he's guilty when he isn't? Could the same be said for others with disabilities or those who find effective communication a struggle?

The policeman on the train is either unaware of Christopher's difficulties or he shows little awareness that he is communicating differently than might be accepted. As

Christopher is groaning whilst being questioned the policeman says, "Young man… stop making that noise…." He is then sarcastic when Christopher fails to stop, "Marvellous." This short sentence stands out on the page and adds emphasis to the sarcastic tone. We, the audience, might assume that someone who has power and authority such as a policeman might have some understanding of differing people's needs but this scene goes to show that actually their job doesn't mean that they have any additional patience when dealing with someone with additional needs. The policeman who arrests Christopher right at the start of the play is similarly unsympathetic so Stephens is certainly highlighting the flaws of adults in power.

In contrast, Ed, Christopher's father, shows far more awareness and acceptance of his disability. He takes into account Christopher's specific preferences, such as his desire to eat foods of a certain colour. He is understanding that seeing four red cars makes the day a "good day" for his son. He is usually a calming influence, remembering that Christopher doesn't like physical touch so he offers his spread fingers as a way of connecting with him and helping Christopher to relax in stressful situations. Structurally, Ed acts as an antidote of sorts to those around Christopher who treat him badly or rudely such as Mrs. Shears and the policeman at the beginning of the play. Stephens shows the audience that it is possible to connect with people like Christopher if you learn what he needs to act and respond in a calm and rational way.

Christopher's mother, Judy, sits somewhere between Ed and Mrs. Shears. She has an understanding of Christopher, connecting with him successfully for the most part, but there are times when she forgets that he is prone to reacting differently, such as when she tries to give him a hug when he arrives to see her in London, before remembering he prefers to use a touching of hands instead. The audience might relate to the difficulties she felt whilst trying to raise her son in Swindon. See the chapter on Judy for further analysis of her relationship with her son.

Acceptance can also apply to Christopher himself as he must accept that his father lied to him and his mother had an affair. He must overcome his initial fear that his father could hurt him if he hurt the dog, "Father had murdered Wellington. That meant he could murder me." For this kind of question it would be worth exploring what Christopher is willing to accept at the start of the play and at the end. There would be plenty to say from his lack of acceptance of physical touch, certain colours etc. through to his eventual ability to accept that his parents have made mistakes. Ultimately do we all reach an acceptance that our parents are only human and not the superheroes we might like them to be? Do we all have differing talents and abilities and levels of acceptance of different abilities?

Another of Christopher's differences to some other children is his love of Maths and Science and his ability to understand them at a high level. The final line highlights his ability rather than disability, "that is how I got an A grade!!!" The exclamation marks highlight Christopher's passion for the subject and how proud he is of his achievement. This is not purely a story of disability, it is far more complex than that. Again we see acceptance from Siobhan, Christopher's teacher, and his father, both of whom support his love of the subjects. In contrast his mother initially tries to postpone him taking the exam for a year. The contrasts can even be seen within Christopher himself as he has the ability to understand complicated scientific theories and yet can't bring himself to eat food of a colour he finds unacceptable.

If an exam answer asks you to focus on the theme of ability and/or disability it would be advisable to use at least two characters in addition to Christopher and explain how they react in different ways when his behaviour is not typical for that of a child of his age. Think also about the effect on an audience; what message is the playwright trying to deliver? The word Autism or Aspergers isn't used at all in the text so it is unlikely to be a study of that one condition but it is certainly a play which explores differing abilities and how people are accepted (or otherwise).

Communication

The nature of different forms of communication and the ways in which our abilities to communicate can help build or maintain relationships with others is a key theme in this play.

From the very start of the play we see ineffective communication from both Mrs. Shears and Christopher. Mrs. Shears opens the play with a question, "What in Christ's name have you done to my dog?" The use of a question involves the audience and the lack of an instant reply from Christopher as they stare at Mrs. Shears' dead dog, Wellington, allows for the audience to consider what may have happened and whether or not Christopher may have been involved. The phrasing "What in Christ's name have you done…" clearly blames Christopher and an audience may find themselves also wrongly assuming Christopher's guilt at this point as a result of the language used by Mrs. Shears. It is possible that Christopher's special needs might also mean that we jump to the wrong conclusions, that he's guilty of this crime that he didn't commit. The audience are also directly addressed at the end of the play, this time by Christopher, whereas in many stage productions the audience are ignored and not communicated with at all.

Mrs. Shears' feelings about the death of Wellington are shown through the breakdown of her language into simple repetition of "Oh no." and "Get away from my dog." The repetition adds emphasis and reveals her initial thoughts that Christopher must be responsible for the demise of her pet.

It is at this point that the style of communication changes and the audience hear from Siobhan, Christopher's teacher, who is reading from the book Christopher has written. The speech beginning "It was seven minutes after midnight…" goes on to narrate the action we are actually seeing on stage. This is a new form of communication again, arguably one which could be confusing for an audience. Christopher's need to pay strict attention to details and facts may initially mean an audience might find him difficult to relate to at the start of the play.

Siobhan is initially expressing Christopher's thoughts when he wrote the book but later in the play we hear from her as Christopher's teacher so she is only partly a narrator of the events. The book Siobhan reads from is similar to a diary as it successfully reveals Christopher's inner thoughts and feelings in a way which can be challenging to achieve on stage. The writing is clear and fairly eloquent in comparison to what we hear on stage during the opening of the play. We learn (through his diary) how the protagonist pays strict attention to details and has a love of facts and figures, "I know all the countries of the world… and every prime number up to 7507". An audience is therefore treated to an insight into the character's thoughts in a way which is usually reserved for novels or possibly achieved through occasional monologues in plays. Despite these extracts being read aloud there remains the problem of a potentially unreliable first person narrator. Despite Christopher insisting, "I do not tell lies," we are hearing this from Christopher himself so cannot be certain of the truth in this statement. The opening of the play does prepare the audience that we will be mainly hearing Christopher's side of the story as the narrative progresses.

 The use of the different voices of Siobhan herself and Christopher through her reading extracts from his book set up a complex system of voices within the play. Not only are there many other characters with speaking roles but there are also voices which can be heard, for example, those which read out the contents of Christopher's pockets when he's at the train station. These are all differing forms of communication received by an audience. This challenging structure could well mirror how Christopher experiences the world; a confusing mix of voices and details which must be sorted through and assembled in logical order. By having to piece together information ourselves an audience may find some of Christopher's struggles easier to relate to.

Not all Autistic people are verbal. Christopher is able to express himself verbally but he has a dislike of metaphors as he prefers to only worry about the literal meaning of everything, "because a pig is not like a day and people do not have skeletons in their cupboards." Again this difficulty could lead to problems with social interaction as people often use figures of speech such as metaphors and they expect the person they are conversing with to understand the metaphor and its meaning. These figures of speech are culturally dependent and have to be learned for their meaning to be understood otherwise the next time someone told you it was "raining cats and dogs outside" I'm sure you would be rushing to the window!

The stage directions in the play are relatively sparse but they do show how Christopher can rely on non-verbal communication to express himself or, in this part of the play, to block out the situation he is finding challenging to deal with (being falsely accused of the murder of Mrs. Shears' dog). "Christopher puts his hands over his ears. He closes his eyes… He starts groaning." Like Mrs. Shears, the stress of the situation has caused Christopher's linguistic abilities to crumble. He resorts to blocking his senses. Christopher relies on physical methods of communication at other points in the play too such as when he gets into a fight with his father, "Ed shakes Christopher hard… Christopher punches Ed repeatedly in the face." Non-verbal communication is also used between Christopher and his parents as due to his dislike of physical touch, they spread their fingers and touch those together instead, rather than giving hugs which might be the preferred means of comfort from other parents to their children. Others with Autism report a similar lack of desire for physical touch and a lack of need for frequent social interaction so the action we are seeing on stage fits with the context of the play.

Whilst sometimes communicating fairly effectively, there are times when Ed also struggles to find the right words to say. At the end of the play as he is most concerned with his need to regain his son's trust, Ed gives a speech which contains repeated use of an ellipsis to show the pauses as he considers how to best express his feelings at this point, "And I... I have to show you that you can trust me... and it will be difficult at first because... because it's a difficult project." Repetition is also used frequently to allow characters to emphasise certain words and phrases, such as "difficult" in the above quote. It is obvious that Ed is indeed going to find it difficult to regain Christopher's trust after he lied to him telling him his mother had died when really she'd had an affair and moved to London. At other times repetition and short sentences are used to show the breakdown of language which mirrors a breakdown of emotions. When, near the end of the play, Ed requests a talk with Christopher his son initially repeats the word "No" seven times. He isn't capable of giving a lengthy explanation as to why he doesn't want to discuss the situation with his father.

In addition to the use of repetition, expletives are also employed to show the strength of feeling of some of the characters at key moments... for example, Ed calls his son a "little shit," and Judy calls Ed a "bastard". This kind of language isn't used regularly in the play so when we do hear it, it is a way of highlighting that situation as being more emotionally charged than others.

In an exam answer be sure to consider the non-verbal forms of communication used (study the stage directions) and think about the tone of voice too – revealed through devices such as punctuation and expletives.

Family tensions and violence

The realisation that our parents are flawed is a tough lesson in the life of any young (or older!) person. Whilst some come to this conclusion early, others may grow up holding their parents in very high esteem and seeing them as role models for themselves as they approach adulthood. For most though, it's fair to say that eventually we see that they are not perfect after all and make mistakes just like anybody else. In Christopher's case he has to come to terms with the fact that neither of his parents has been trustworthy and their actions have undermined his previous faith in them. The fallibility of adults is a recurring theme in the play.

Christopher's father, Ed, has been secretive about what really happened when Christopher's mother Judy had an affair with Mr. Shears and left the family home to live in London. When Christopher discovers the truth the stage directions state that his "thrashing has exhausted him." The verb "thrashing" here suggests that Christopher's behaviour has been out of control. He has also been sick so the mental trauma of realising he has been lied to by his father has taken a physical toll on him. When his father finds him in a ball on the floor with the letters next to him he uses short sentences and expletives to emphasise his strength of feeling when he finds out his father lied about his mother's death, "These are. Oh shit. Oh Christ." Ed doesn't respond in such an extreme, physical way like Christopher but he does lose his eloquence and struggle to find the words to respond. The playwright uses ellipses in the short speech which follows to show how Ed is struggling to explain his actions, "I don't know what to say… I was in such a mess… I said she was in hospital." This is not the only time we see the use of this form of punctuation as Ed struggles to express himself. The technique is seen again near the end of the play when he is trying to apologise and explain his realisation that he needs his son to trust him again, "And I… I have to show you that you can trust me… and it will be difficult at first because… because it's a difficult project." The repetition of the technique means it is something you should look out for in an extract question too, if that's the kind of question your exam board sets for this text.

Judy Boone's actions have also contributed to the break-up of Christopher's family. It would seem the move to London hasn't solved all the issues either as she is seen arguing with Mr. Shears. In her letters she says that she thinks she was "not a very good mother." She believes Christopher is "much calmer" around his father and explains how she "decided it would be better for all of us if I went." Her language suggests that her move to London wasn't actually as selfish as it may have first appeared, "better for all of us" leads an audience to believe that she might have actually been trying to improve the situation for Christopher.

Judy had a difficult time with Christopher's behaviour, even having her toes broken when Christopher threw a chopping board which hit her foot. She says she "couldn't walk properly for a month." Judy's language appears calm and considered, no doubt because having chosen the form of a letter (rather than a phone call or face-to-face conversation where there is less time to think and plan a response.) She has had time to consider exactly which words to use. Her coherent and clear sentences can be compared to Ed's expletives and broken sentences when the ellipses which have already been mentioned are used. Through his use of language and punctuation the playwright shows a clear difference in the style of communication during the time when the family tensions and outcomes are being revealed to Christopher.

The tensions between Ed and his father become violent early on in the play, "Ed shakes Christopher hard… Christopher punches Ed repeatedly in the face." The verbs "shakes" and "punches" show differing forms of violence. The violent verbs here can be analysed in more depth. Arguably the shaking is slightly less severe than the punching as there is no direct impact. Perhaps Ed as the father is less inclined to react in a way that will actually cause damage to his son whereas Christopher's punches show less control and more desire to hurt his dad. The adverb "repeatedly" again shows the strength of feeling between the two and the loss of control on Christopher's part. The theme is revisited as Christopher's book (read by Siobhan) reveals, "Father had murdered Wellington. That meant he could murder me." The word "murder" suggests a planned attack designed to deliberately kill. The use of alliteration in "murder me" is memorable. Instead of being able to go to his parents in times of difficulty and stress, Christopher is having to run away. He repeats "I had to get out of the house" five times. This use of repetition by the playwright could show Christopher's inability to get past that one thought in his mind. It's all he can think about in that mind so the line is repeated until he can move on. The book being read by Siobhan shows what is happening in Christopher's mind, things that he might not always be able to express verbally. He also uses the action of pointing a Swiss Army knife at his father when Ed arrives in London to communicate his violent thoughts surrounding his father's betrayal. This gesture would no doubt be quite shocking when seen on stage. Don't forget to look out for the stage directions and learn quotes from these as well as the lines which are actually delivered.

By the end of the play the family tensions are some way to being resolved. Christopher and his father are reunited in Swindon and focuses on them both rebuilding a relationship. Judy remains in London but Christopher appears accepting of her and the future seems to be positive for the family, despite the remaining separation.

A Postmodern Approach To The Play

Postmodernism is usually more of an A level concept (feel free to do some background reading about it) but there are two techniques used in postmodern texts that are also found in *Curious Incident* so it seems worthy of mention.

Firstly, an aspect often found in postmodern texts is intertextuality. This is where an existing text is referenced in the new one. Take Shrek for example, this relies on the audience's prior knowledge of fairytale characters and the fairytale genre to work. In *Curious Incident* Stafania Ciocia in her paper entitled "The Curious Incident of the Dog in the Night-time and Detective Fictions" mentions how the title is actually a quotation from *Silver Blaze*, one of the adventures of Sherlock Holmes. In addition, the presence of the dog also appears to be a reference to one of Sherlock Holmes' most famous inventions, *The Hound of the Baskervilles*. Of course, without prior knowledge of these other stories and characters, the audience is unaffected by these references.

Ciocia also explains how *Curious Incident* can actually be seen as an "anti-detective" story. She explains that, unlike classic detective fiction, Christopher "stumbles upon" the solution to the mystery of who killed Wellington, she also believes he is "clueless and doomed to failure" unlike most heroes of detective fiction.

Postmodern texts don't necessarily stick faithfully to one genre. We frequently see aspects of more than one genre appearing. Take "rom coms" for example which combine romance with comedy, or we can even see combinations of horror and comedy in films such as *Shaun of the Dead*. *Curious Incident* is certainly part detective story… first we have Christopher setting out to find the killer of Mrs. Shears's dog but in doing so he uncovers the second mystery… that of what actually happened to his mother Judy. However, the story could also be described as a psychological drama. It is arguably as much a study of how Christopher deals with the world as an Autistic person and an analysis of how others respond to him when he behaves in an atypical way, as it is crime fiction. All of these different ways of "reading" the play (or the novel) depend on what the reader brings to the table via their own experiences. Someone who is familiar with Autism may offer a very different approach to someone who has never met an Autistic person. The level of sympathy for Christopher and his parents might well depend on each audience member's approach to the context.

Key differences to the original novel by Mark Haddon

The play version is very true to the original novel but it is worth mentioning some key differences. Obviously seeing the play on stage allows the playwright to fill in the gaps in the text about what the characters look like and how they express themselves. If you have previously read the novel be very careful that you focus entirely on the play version in your exam. Here are some other notable differences:

- Characters are able to speak for themselves rather than us hearing from them mainly through Christopher and his book.
- In the novel the whole text is the book which Christopher has written. In the play we hear extracts from the book (read aloud by Siobhan) whilst we see live action on stage.
- We hear directly from the characters on stage which adds weight to what they say. The novel is told primarily from Christopher's point of view. Hearing from characters directly adds weight to what they say, it doesn't feel as if Christopher has filtered their words as could be the case in the novel.
- There are different voices used which inform the audience of specific details.
- Stage directions are used in the script to explain the physical actions of characters. These should never be overlooked when analysing the play as stage directions are a key component of the play form.
- The novel is primarily narrative whereas the play relies on dialogue.

Other than that, the themes and the characters remain the same. Reading the novel would be useful but you mustn't forget that your text set for study is the play. Do see the stage production if you can. Be careful to always refer to it as a PLAY and talk about the AUDIENCE, rather than "readers." This will ensure that you are always gaining marks for talking about the correct form.

Ways of remembering the plot

If you need help remembering the plot or storyline of the text you could try mapping it out. Draw the journey Christopher takes, drawing a picture for each main event but then link each picture to a journey you already know very well, say from your house to your school. Link each of the main events in the play to a landmark you know on your own journey.

For example, the play starts with Christopher, Mrs. Shears and the dead dog in Mrs. Shears' garden. Imagine that scene is taking place in your own garden.

Next Christopher goes to the police station – which landmark do you pass on your way to school? Could the police station be the bus stop near your house? Or a park down the road? Or a pub?

You get the idea…. Your school could be London! To recall the order of events in an exam just imagine your journey again and it should help you to remember events in the correct order. This can be done with any text, not just *Curious Incident.*

Scene	Summary	Characters	Location
1	Dead dog, Mrs. Shears' garden	Mrs. Shears, Chris	My front lawn
2	Police station	Chris, policeman	Bus stop over the road

It doesn't matter if the place in the story is repeated (e.g. Christopher's house). It's the event/scene that you need to remember so still assign it a new spot on your own journey.

KEY QUOTATIONS (and ways to learn them):

If you are studying *Curious Incident* for a G.C.S.E. exam, it is very likely that you will be sitting a "closed book" examination. This means that you will not be able to take a copy of the text with you into the exam. As a result, you will need to memorise a number of quotations to use within your exam answer. When choosing quotations to memorise, it is essential to think carefully about the major themes contained within the text. The quotes you learn should be flexible – so they might be good to use for both a character and one or two themes or techniques. Let's look at some examples:

Q: Explore how Stephens presents the character of Ed Boone.

This question does not explicitly mention any themes, but we know from this guide that Ed Boone links most strongly to the themes of truth/lies, communication and family relationships.

Relevant quotes here might include:

- **"Don't give me that bollocks you little shit."** – This quote is easy to remember due to the swearing, it could be used to comment on communication, so the playwright's use of language (expletives) and used for the themes of family relationships and truth and lies.

- **"Ed shakes Christopher hard… Christopher punches Ed repeatedly in the face."** – this quote is from the stage directions; by including it we are showing we understand the form of the text is a play and we're aware of the devices playwrights use. Again the themes include the use of communication but this time non-verbal, plus family relationships of course.

- **"mate"** – Here Ed uses informal language. It effectively supports the point that the family relationships are not all negative and that there is a clear bond between Ed and his son.

- **"I have to show you that you can trust me."** – If you mention that this quote appears at the end of the play you are including references to the play's structure. It also suggests the family relationship between Ed and Christopher appears to be improving as Ed attempts to reconnect after the lies he has previously told about Christopher's mother, the dog and his own relationship with Mrs. Spears.

Those 4 quotes are worth learning (as are most of the quotes contained in this ebook but you may need to be a bit selective). These specifically could be used for questions on Ed and Christopher as well as on themes of communication, truth/lies and family relationships. You should also consider both how easy the actual quote itself is to remember – swear words and violence tend to be quite memorable but you will need others that you find easy to remember too so that you cover a wide range of possible questions.

Once in the exam... the first couple of minutes!

Before you begin you answer once you're in the exam jot down any quotes which you can remember that might be relevant to an answer. This is particularly applicable if you just have a question and no extract but even answers on an extract should reference other events and moments in the play. If in doubt write them down, you don't have to use them in your essay if they turn out to be irrelevant (don't crowbar them in there just because you went to the trouble of learning them!) but at least you can relax and stop trying to remember them. If others spring to mind, add those to the list too.

Do make sure your answer remains relevant to the question. DO NOT go off on a different tangent because those are the only quotes you can remember! You will be rewarded for your knowledge of the play even if the quotes you use are few and far between or if you can't remember the exact wording. Do make attempts to learn as many as you can though.

So how do I remember all these quotes you say I need?

Learning quotes be done in many different ways...

Revision Cards

 Try writing out the whole quote on one side of your paper. On the other side write out all but the end. Aim to remember the last word or two when you go back to revise it.

Christopher punches Ed repeatedly in the ????

If you remember, take away more words until you just have the first word (or not even that!)

Christopher punches ?? ?? ?? ?? ??

Repetition is the key. Keep going with the exercises until you are confident you can remember the quotes. There is no quick fix unfortunately. It's hard work but it'll be worth it when you're in the exam.

Using your phone or laptop

You can also use technology to help you. Make a summary of the text using only key quotes, pictures and music. Use an app on your phone or computer to add the pictures and music to help you remember. Just looking at the quote often (as you edit the piece) will help, plus you might find the image easy to remember and the quote may just go with it in your mind." I have had students learn large numbers of quotes this way. They have produced some stunning work. An example is this photostory about the lengthy poem Rime of the Ancient Mariner: the students who produced this memorised many of the quotes they used as they were editing it.

<u>If you're an artist…</u>

You might prefer to draw images to go with your quotes. The time it takes you to draw the picture and the addition of details might well help you to remember the quote. You are only then really remembering one image rather than several words.

<u>Using acronyms</u>

Alternatively you could list quotes, making words down the side as you do so (like an acrostic poem). I used to do this for my A level and Degree studies. I would condense my notes into a list of key points (or quotes) then learn the word (or words) down the side and what each letter stood for. When I got into the exam the first thing I would do before I even looked at any questions was to write down my lists. It would take about 5 minutes (you can list quite a few points in 5 mins) and I could then pick and choose what was relevant from the list for my actual answer. If I forgot what any letters stood for in the heat of the moment I left them blank as I might remember them during the course of the exam once the adrenaline had subsided.

So for the quotes above you might learn the word **DIME** (a small coin).

"**D**on't give me that bollocks you little shit."

"**I** have to show you that you can trust me."

"**m**ate"

"**E**d shakes Christopher hard… Christopher punches Ed repeatedly in the face."

Of course you don't have to use the first word… you might want:

Bollocks, Trust, Mate and Punch as key words from the quote.

You might conjure up a picture of a man punching his mate in the… well you know… over a trust issue (had an affair with his wife?!) Or you could make up a saying with the letters B, T, M and P like "Ma and Pa Bake Tarts."

<u>Which quotes can be used for which characters and themes?</u>

All of the following quotes can be analysed for the playwright's use of language but below is a suggestion of which quotes could be used for different themes, characters and questions. "Context" refers to how the quote could be linked to Christopher's Autism and would also link to any question on ability/disability. Which other quotes/themes have you studied that you could add?

Quote	Should link to the characters/themes:
"dog was dead"	Structure (opening – sets up the mystery), alliteration
"that is how I got an A grade!!!"	Christopher, structure (end, addressing the audience)
"Get away from my dog."	Mrs. Shears, communication, structure (opening).
"After twelve and a half minutes a policeman arrived."	Christopher communication, context (precise recall of details).
"I really like little spaces so long as there is no one else in them with me."	Christopher, context
"I would have to talk to other people from Mission Control, but we would do that through a radio link-up and a TV monitor so it wouldn't be like real people who are strangers but it would be like playing a computer game."	Christopher, communication, context.
"I find people confusing."	Christopher communication, context.
"it's red food colouring because I don't eat yellow food."	Christopher, context
"because a pig is not like a day and people do not have skeletons in their cupboards."	Christopher, communication (metaphors), truth, context.
"Don't give me that bollocks you little shit."	Ed, communication (expletives), family tensions.
"Ed shakes Christopher hard… Christopher punches Ed repeatedly in the face." mate"	Christopher, Ed, communication, family tensions/violence.
"I think that can be very easily arranged."	Christopher, Ed, context (Ed is happy to accommodate Christopher's wish to eat broccoli and beans for tea).
"Your father is a much	Judy, Ed, communication, family tensions,

more patient person."	alliteration.
"You being in the house but refusing to talk to me."	Ed, Christopher, communication, context.
"No…"	Ed, Christopher, context (When Ed tries to talk to Christopher he repeats "no" seven times).
"Siobhan says that if you raise one eyebrow it can mean lots of different things. It can mean 'I want to do sex with you.' I never said that."	Christopher, Siobhan, communication, context.
"If you say you don't want to do it no one is going to be angry with you."	Siobhan, family tensions.
"it's because I'm not your mother."	Siobhan, family tensions.
"What in Christ's name have you done to my dog?"	Mrs. Shears, communication, truth/lies.
"I mean they were very good friends. Very, very good friends."	Family tensions, truth/lies.
"not a very good mother".	Judy, family tensions.
"Much calmer"	Ed, Judy, family tensions.
"cried and cried and cried"	Judy, family tensions, repetition.
"decided it would be better for all of us if I went"	Judy, family tensions.
"Love" "sweetheart" Put together as they're used by Judy at the same time in the same way.	Judy, Christopher, communication, family tensions.
"Bastard. The Bastard"	Ed, Judy, family tensions, communication.
"Young man… stop making that noise…."	Policeman, Christopher, context, communication.
"Marvellous."	Policeman, Christopher, context, communication.
"And I… I have to show	Ed, Christopher, communication, punctuation

you that you can trust me… and it will be difficult at first because… because it's a difficult project."	(ellipses), structure (ending).
"good day"	Christopher, context.
"Oh no."	Mrs. Shears, communication.
"It was seven minutes after midnight…"	Christopher communication, context (precise recall of details).
"I know all the countries of the world… and every prime number up to 7507."	Christopher communication, truth/lies (facts) context (precise recall of details).
"I do not tell lies,"	Christopher, communication, truth/lies.
"Christopher puts his hands over his ears. He closes his eyes… He starts groaning."	Christopher, communication, context.
"thrashing has exhausted him."	Christopher, verbs, context, family tensions.
"These are. Oh shit. Oh Christ."	Ed, communication (short sentences and expletives).
"I don't know what to say… I was in such a mess… I said she was in hospital."	Ed, truth/lies (about Judy), communication, family tensions.
"Father had murdered Wellington. That meant he could murder me."	Christopher, context, truth/lies.
"I had to get out of the house"	Christopher, context, family tensions.
"Not all murders are solved Christopher. Not all murderers are caught."	Siobhan, truth/lies.
"Then I detected in the utility room. Then I detected in the dining room. Then I detected in the living room…"	Christopher, repetition, truth/lies, communication.

"You are to stop this ridiculous bloody detective game right now."	Christopher, Ed, truth/lies, expletives and adjectives (language).
"I am going to tell you the truth from now on. About everything…."	Ed, truth/lies, communication, family tensions, structure (end).
"It's going to be all right. Honestly. Trust me."	Ed, truth/lies, communication, family tensions, structure (end).
"howls"	Judy, communication, truth/lies, family tensions.
"If you try any of that monkey-business again, you little shit, I am going to seriously lose my rag."	Policeman, communication, expletives and metaphors (language).
"The rain looks like white sparks."	Christopher, simile (language), context.
"this flat is hardly big enough for two people."	Mr. Shears, family tensions.
"You've got a bloody nerve."	Mrs. Shears, family tensions.
"couldn't walk properly for a month."	Judy, family tensions, Christopher, context.

As I have stated elsewhere, you should also aim to include **at least one stage direction** – this will make it clear to the examiner that you are aware of the play form.

ANSWERING EXAM QUESTIONS

Different exam boards have different ways of presenting exam questions. Some print an extract from the text, others ask broader questions e.g. on themes or characters. Let's start with an extract question. Imagine the first two pages of the play have been copied and include the first stage direction, "A dead dog…" up to Christopher's answer to the policeman, "I'm fifteen years and three months and two days."

Q: How does Stephens present different forms of communication in this extract from *The Curious Incident of the Dog in the Night-Time.*

from:

 Mrs. Shears: What in Christ's name have you done to my dog?

To

 Christopher: I think someone killed the dog.

Write about:

- **The different ways in which the characters communicate in this extract**

- **How Stephens presents the attitudes and feelings of the characters at this point in the play via their communication skills.**

You should be able to spot where the extract is from in the play. The key phrase here is, 'how does Simon Stephens present'. The question is NOT 'what is Christopher like', but instead it focuses on how he presented by the playwright. The word 'presented' can be read as 'use language, structure, form and context'. (Do check that your exam board assesses context as not all do).

After writing down any quotations you want to be able to forget about and reference later, I would suggest you create a brief plan in which you map out these four (or three) areas of your answer. Make sure you annotate the extract, picking out your key quotations and bearing in mind your need to focus on the language, structure, form and possibly context before you begin writing your answer.

You should link the extract to other events in the play to show your understanding of the whole text (this is where your learned quotations can make an appearance) but be careful not to start retelling the whole story or writing an answer focusing on only one theme or character unless that's what was asked for. Read the question several times until you are sure of exactly what is being asked of you. This planning time is built into the exam time. No examiner expects you (or wants you) to begin writing your answer from the second the invigilator tells you to turn your paper over!

No matter what the question, the best way of ensuring you stay focused on the question is to PLAN before you begin writing and check back over your plan regularly as you complete your answer. You MUST avoid writing several paragraphs which you later realise (or worse, don't realise!) are irrelevant to the question being asked. It is the temptation of many students to write as quickly as they can about as much as they can remember but you will not gain marks for additional analysis which does not address the actual question posed by the exam board.

Your plan for the above question might look something like this (although it may be written in even shorter note form and contain more quotes.)

Language: Repetition – Mrs. Spears grief over the death of Wellington "Oh no. Oh no."

"dog was dead" – alliteration, memorable.

Structure: Christopher's inner thoughts revealed by Siobhan reading from his book. Precise descriptions. Audience struggle to piece together info (like Chris).

Clear and eloquent in contrast to the actual action on stage, "After twelve and a half minutes a policeman arrived."

Problems with Christopher as a potentially unreliable first person narrator, "I do not tell lies."

Form: Play – use of stage directions. Breakdown of language when Christopher is struggling with a situation. Non-verbal communication in the stage directions reveal his feelings, "Christopher puts his hands over his ears. He closes his eyes… He starts groaning."

Context: Christopher- on the Autistic Spectrum so finds verbal communication during unpredictable confrontations challenging. Exclusion of outsiders.

Most exams allow 45 minutes to one hour for a question on Curious Incident.

Sample Answer:

Simon Stephens uses language, structure and form and context to present differing forms of communication used by the characters in the opening two pages of *The Curious Incident of the Dog in the Night-Time*.

Communication is a key theme within the play and the differing ways in which characters communicate is clear from the very start. Mrs. Shears opens the play with a question, "What in Christ's name have you done to my dog?" The use of a question involves the audience and the lack of an instant reply from Christopher allows for the audience to consider what may have happened as they stare at Mrs. Shears' dead dog Wellington and whether or not Christopher may have been involved. This question also sets up the "whodunit" style of the play so this opening question is arguably the playwright communicating the play's intentions to the audience as much as it is Mrs. Shears asking Christopher what his involvement was with the death of her dog. Mrs. Shears' use of language reveals her assumption that Christopher killed her dog. This assumption could just be based on him standing in her garden over the dead dog or it could be she is aware of his potential for violent outbursts. Either way she gives him little chance to explain and is clearly intolerant of his disability. The question engages an audience who may also assume that Christopher was responsible for the dog's death, either due to his inability to explain himself or because of Mrs. Shears' wording which implies he was to blame, "What in Christ's name have YOU done…" Upon realising that Christopher actually had nothing to do with the death of the dog it is up to an audience to reflect on whether or not they had jumped to the incorrect conclusion too.

Mrs. Shears' feelings about the death of Wellington are shown through the breakdown of her language into simple repetition of "Oh no." and "Get away from my dog." The repetition adds emphasis to her words and emphasises her initial thoughts that Christopher must be responsible for the demise of her pet.

It is at this point that the style of communication changes and the audience hear from Siobhan, Christopher's teacher, who is reading from the book Christopher has written. The speech beginning "It was seven minutes after midnight…" and goes on to narrate the action we are actually seeing on stage. This is a new form of communication again, arguably one which could be confusing for an audience. Siobhan is initially expressing Christopher's thoughts when he wrote the book but later in the play we hear from her as Christopher's teacher so she is only partly a narrator of the events. The structure is also complex as we are watching a scene which must have already happened as Christopher has already written about it in his book. The audience have to work hard to piece together the information as it's revealed, just as Christopher has to work hard to understand the forms of communication coming his way too. This complex structure really challenges the audience as Stephens encourages them to sympathise with Christopher's situation.

The book Siobhan reads from is similar to a diary as it successfully reveals Christopher's inner thoughts and feelings in a way which can be challenging to achieve on stage. The writing is clear and fairly eloquent in comparison to what we hear on stage during the opening of the play. We learn (through his diary) how the protagonist pays strict attention to details and has a love of facts and figures, "I know all the countries of the world… and every prime number up to 7507". This fits with the context of the play as Christopher is on the Autistic Spectrum and has a love of facts and figures. An audience is therefore treated to an insight into his thoughts in a way which is usually reserved for novels or possibly achieved through occasional monologues in plays. This could be off-putting though as an audience may not relate to his obsession with correct details. Stephens presents Christopher as an intriguing character who we may sympathise with at times but also struggle to understand his methods of making the world accessible for himself.

Despite these extracts being read aloud there remains the problem of a potentially unreliable first person narrator. Despite Christopher insisting, "I do not tell lies," we are hearing from Christopher himself so cannot be certain of the truth of what we are hearing. This opening does, however, prepare the audience that we will be hearing mainly his side of the story as the narrative progresses.

The stage directions in the play are relatively sparse but they do show how Christopher can rely on non-verbal communication to express himself or, in this part of the play, to block out the situation he is finding challenging to deal with (being falsely accused of the murder of Mrs. Shears' dog). "Christopher puts his hands over his ears. He closes his eyes… He starts groaning." Like Mrs. Shears, the stress of the situation has caused Christopher's linguistic abilities to crumble. He resorts to blocking his senses. It is these moments in the play that may make it difficult for the audience to see Christopher as a reliable narrator as he clearly misses chances for communication when he cannot cope with the situation. He does claim later in the play, "I do not tell lies," but the forms of non-verbal communication used in this extract do make it clear that he is a potentially inadequate narrator at best. Christopher relies on physical methods of communication at other points in the play too such as when he later gets into a fight with his father, "Ed shakes Christopher hard… Christopher punches Ed repeatedly in the face."

We continue to hear his voice through Siobhan's readings but Christopher's actual voiced comments on stage are very simple and to the point as he responds to the officer, "I think someone killed the dog." The playwright highlights how inside Christopher thinks in far more depth, even noticing the orange leaf on the shoe of the policeman who arrives, but he doesn't actually verbalise all that he is thinking. Maybe the message to an audience is not to underestimate those who are quieter or who are less keen to discuss their private thoughts and feelings.

Later in the play we learn about Christopher's other abilities in subject areas such as Maths and Science. It would appear that Stephens uses the character of Christopher to encourage the audience to question how understanding they are of others' abilities and disabilities. The struggles of the characters to communicate are highlighted even from these opening two pages of the play. Mrs. Shears is unable to voice her thoughts fully and Christopher relies mainly on non-verbal communication during those first two pages. It is only through Siobhan that more of his true character is revealed. The use of the different voices of Siobhan herself and Christopher through her reading extracts from his book sets up a complex system of voices which is extended when we hear other voices on stage later in the play, such as the variety of voices which read out the contents of his pockets when he's at the train station. The voices are a structural device which help to drive the narrative action. The first two pages of the play effectively prepare the audience for the variety of ways in which we will learn about the characters and their abilities to communicate as the rest of the story progresses.

Of course your exam board might not use printed extracts so here's a question focusing on a theme instead…

Q. How does the playwright present the theme of truth in *The Curious Incident of the Dog in the Night-Time"?*

Remember the same rules about planning to include structure, form, language and possibly context still apply. Jot down your quotes in advance so you have a selection to choose from. Have a look at the earlier chapters of this ebook for ways of remembering key quotes.

The first line – you can learn this!

An effective way to start this essay is with the following sentence: **Simon Stephens uses language, structure and form and context to present the theme of truth in "The Curious Incident of the Dog in the Night-Time."**

None of the exam boards actually award marks for introductions or conclusions. As a result, they should be brief. My one sentence introduction is deceptively simple. In fact, it achieves a great deal to impress the examiner:

It shows that I am aware the play and its characters are not real.

It identifies the four prongs of successful analysis: language, structure, form and context. Many pupils will fail to address all four, but by pointing them out in the introduction, you are making it very clear to the examiner that you will be writing a comprehensive answer.

Sample Answer

Simon Stephens uses language, structure and form and context to present the theme of   truth in *The Curious Incident of the Dog in the Night-Time.*

Christopher likes the truth. He sets out at the start of the play to find out who killed Wellington the dog. We find out early on that he doesn't like metaphors because he sees them as a form of lie, "because a pig is not like a day and people do not have skeletons in their cupboards." Like many people with Autism, Christopher struggles to infer meaning so can find sarcasm and figures of speech difficult.

It is perhaps unsurprising that Christopher favours subjects such as Science and Maths as those tend to have correct answers. It is rarely down to a matter of opinion so the outcomes are predictable and Christopher finds comfort in that certainty "I know all the countries of the world… and every prime number up to 7507". 1+1 will always equal 2, whereas people's opinions are changeable. Christopher's obsession with the fine details may make him difficult for an audience to relate to, especially at the start of the play.

Christopher says, "I do not tell lies" and even from the opening of the play we see his search for the truth but at this stage it is focused on solving the mystery of who killed Wellington the dog. Ed tries to prevent Christopher's search for answers, "You are to stop this ridiculous bloody detective game right now." The use of the expletive here foreshadows Ed's involvement with the murder. At this point in the play he is desperate for his lies about his wife who is actually alive in London and his killing of

Wellington to remain uncovered. It is Siobhan who reminds Christopher, "Not all murders are solved Christopher. Not all murderers are caught." The repetition of "Not all" adds emphasis to the lines and reminds the audience that honesty does not always prevail. Despite these characters whom Christopher is close to trying to prevent him, the playwright shows his strength of character (despite his disability) to persevere and try to find the person responsible for Wellington's demise.

Christopher is quite determined when it comes to uncovering the truth. When his father has taken his book Christopher starts a search. Ironically we hear of this when Siobhan reads from his book. "Then I detected in the utility room. Then I detected in the dining room. Then I detected in the living room…" The use of repetition here shows how Christopher is stuck in this train of thought and is wholly focused on finding the book. In trying to solve that mystery Christopher finds the first letter from his mother addressed to him so he actually uncovers another mystery. This structure drives the plot as the audience wonder who killed the dog, where the book has been hidden and now what is the situation with the letters and what is the truth about Christopher's mother.

Ed is a character who realises the error of lying, in this case to his son about what happened with Judy. We see Ed's character development from someone who has successfully kept the secret that his wife is alive and well and living in London, to someone who regrets this deceitful behaviour, "I am going to tell you the truth from now on. About everything.…" He goes on to admit killing the dog and lying about what happened to Judy, "I don't know what to say… I was in such a mess… I said she was in hospital." Ed's choice of words after this admission suggest he is determined to right the wrongs which have been done but it is possible to think it unlikely that Christopher will be able to move past this easily, "It's going to be all right. Honestly. Trust me." The use of short sentences again sums up the feelings of the character. All he wants to be in this moment is finally honest with his son. There could be a lesson in the text for an audience; lying only gets you into trouble.

When Judy first hears of the lies Ed has been telling Christopher about her the stage directions say she "howls." This verb is one most associated with animals such as wolves. It is as if the thought of her son thinking she has died causes Judy to act in an animalistic way. Just as we've seen with other characters throughout the course of the play the lies stop her from being able to communicate and use language effectively. She resorts to expletives to describe Ed, "Bastard. The Bastard." The use of capital letters and the addition of the word "The" makes it seem as if she has given Ed a derogatory title in response to the lies he has been telling about her.

In contrast, Siobhan never lies to Christopher. Christopher asks her repeatedly, "Does that mean I can do anything?" and she never actually answers the question as to do so would either be a lie (if she told Christopher he could, indeed, do anything) or it might crush Christopher's hopes, dreams and potentially damage his self-esteem if she was to let him know that no, he cannot do absolutely anything. Both Christopher and Siobhan are characters who strive to tell the truth even in difficult circumstances and so therefore can be admired by an audience.

By the end of the play many truths have been revealed, not only that Ed was the person who actually killed Wellington but also that Judy is alive and had an affair with Mr. Shears which turned into a relationship which she is still in. The mysteries and revelation of the truths drive the plot and it is impossible to ignore the message that "cheats never prosper."

CHECK YOUR UNDERSTANDING – THE ANSWERS!

Check your understanding: Christopher Boone

1. What form of Autism does Christopher have?

Asperger's Syndrome

2. Why does Christopher prefer subjects like Maths and Science over English?

Subjects like Science and Maths have facts and right and wrong answers, unlike English.

3. How does Christopher react when Mrs. Shears tells him to get away from her dead dog?

He closes his eyes, puts his hands over his ears and groans.

4. Why might some people with Autism find it easier to communicate with other people over the internet or via text message?

People with Autism often find it hard to read facial expressions and emotions, which can make face-to-face conversations more challenging.

5. How does the communication and connection Christopher has with Siobhan differ to that which he has with his father?

When talking to his father Christopher's mind wanders, for example when his dad is apologising, Christopher is wondering where his book is. In contrast he is closer to Siobhan, he chats with her about his mother, his interests and things that are worrying him.

6. Who does Christopher want to live with at the end of the play?

Siobhan (but she refuses).

7. Which two colours does Christopher dislike?

Yellow and brown

8. Why doesn't Christopher like metaphors?

Christopher sees metaphors as a kind of lie and he likes the truth.

9. Why does Christopher become afraid of his father?

Christopher finds out his father killed Wellington the dog so he thinks his father could kill him too.

10. How is Christopher's self-esteem by the end of the play?

Christopher's self-esteem has improved after he has overcome some significant challenges such as travelling alone to London and solving the mystery of who killed Wellington.

Check your understanding: Ed Boone

1. What is Ed's relationship status at the start of the play?

Ed is separated from his wife (Christopher's mother) and has been in a relationship with Mrs. Spears.

2. What are the similarities between Ed and his son?

Ed and Christopher both struggle with communication, can both react angrily and both react physically to stressful situations.

3. Give an example of Ed's use of expletives when he's talking to Christopher…

"Don't give me that bollocks you little shit."

4. What lies do we find out Ed has been telling Christopher?

Ed has been telling his son that Christopher's mother has died. He also doesn't reveal that actually she left him and had an affair, or that he was the one who killed Wellington the dog.

5. What does Ed call his son which suggests he sometimes sees him as a friend?

"Mate."

6. How does Judy describe Ed in comparison to herself?

Judy describes Ed as a "patient person."

7. Who has Ed been having an affair with?

Mrs. Shears

8. How has the situation between Ed and Christopher improved by the end of the play?

Ed says he is proud of Christopher at the end of the play and he seems determined to improve their relationship.

9. What does the writer's repeated use of ellipses during Ed's speech near the end of the play reveal about Ed's state of mind at this time?

The repeated use of the ellipses suggests that Ed has to pause and think carefully about which words to use to improve the relationship with his son.

10. What is Ed determined to do by the end of the play?

Ed is determined to rebuild his relationship with Christopher.

Check your understanding: Judy Boone

1. What does Christopher believe has happened to his mother at the start of the play?

Christopher believes that his mother has died (as that's the explanation his father gave him, when actually his mother had left and had an affair with Mr. Spears).

2. At which point in the play does Christopher realise that his father has been lying to him about his mother?

When Christopher finds the letters his mother has been sending him.

3. How does Christopher remember his mother when he thinks about their past relationship?

Christopher remembers his mother as someone who got cross with him and struggled to handle the specifics of his condition.

4. Which character told Christopher that his mother had been having an affair with Mr. Spears?

Mrs. Alexander.

5. Where is Judy actually living and who with?

Judy is living in London with Mr. Spears.

6. What does Judy think of her own parenting skills?

She thought she was "not a good mother." She thought Christopher was better off with his Dad and recalls crying after a particularly difficult day.

7. When she first sees Christopher again, how does Judy do try to greet him (which Christopher doesn't appreciate?)

Judy tries to hug him before remembering he doesn't like that.

8. What does she do next to greet him more successfully?

Judy remembers to spread he fingers and reach out to Christopher and touch his hands that way.

9. What does Judy call her son which shows she really does care for him?

"Love" and "sweetheart."

10. What does Judy call Ed when he finds out he has been lying to Christopher and saying she'd died?

"Bastard."

Check your understanding: Siobhan

1. Who is Siobhan and how does she know Christopher?

Siobhan is Christopher's teacher.

2. How old is Siobhan?

Siobhan is 27.

3. How does Siobhan act as a narrator as well as a character in her own right?

Siobhan reads from Christopher's book and so is narrating the action we see on stage at times (e.g. at the beginning of the play.)

4. Which other texts does Siobhan read from during the play?

Siobhan reads from the letters which Judy sent to Christopher.

5. Give an example of other voices used in the play…

Voices 1-6 which reveal the contents of Christopher's pockets.

6. How does Siobhan act as a mother figure to Christopher?

Siobhan offers Christopher support and understanding and sees how his achievements in Maths give him self-confidence so she encourages this.

7. Why does Siobhan adopt the role of a mother figure to Christopher?

Siobhan adopts the role of a mother to Christopher as his own mother isn't present (Christopher believes her to be dead.)

8. Siobhan supports Christopher's decision to sit his Maths A level but what does she say to him to try and avoid putting unnecessary pressure on him?

She says, "If you don't want to no one is going to be angry with you."

9. Why doesn't Siobhan let Christopher go and live with her at the end of the play?

Siobhan says, "It's because I'm not your mother." She never acts as an actual replacement for Judy.

10. How much do we know about Siobhan's own life or background beyond her relationship and support for Christopher?

Very little, Siobhan is used as a dramatic device in the play.

Check your understanding: Minor Characters

1. Who is Mrs. Alexander?

Mrs. Alexander is an elderly neighbour of Christopher's.

2. How does Mrs. Alexander treat Christopher?

She is kind to him.

3. What important information does Mrs. Alexander reveal to Christopher?

Mrs. Alexander tells Christopher that his mother had an affair with Mr. Spears.

4. Where is Mr. Spears now?

Mr. Spears is living in London with Christopher's mother, Judy.

5. Who owns the dog which has died at the start of the play?

Mrs. Shears

6. How does Mr. Shears react when Christopher arrives at their London flat?

Mr. Spears isn't keen for Christopher to stay as he says, "this flat is hardly big enough for two people."

7. Why did Ed kill Wellington the dog?

Ed's relationship with Mrs. Shears had gone sour.

8. Who did Mrs. Shears first blame for he death of her dog?

Mrs. Shears blamed Christopher for the death of her dog Wellington at the start of the play.

9. How do the policemen Christopher meets treat him?

The policemen treat Christopher without the respect and understanding you might expect. They even swear at him.

10. What other animal (belonging to Christopher) do we meet during the play?

We meet Christopher's pet rat, Toby.

GLOSSARY:

Adjectives: Words which modify nouns, also known as 'describing words'. They may form a list as in "**ridiculous, bloody** detective game."

Adverb: A word which is used to add meaning to or change the meaning of a verb, adjective, another verb or clause. For example, "Christopher punches Ed **repeatedly**."

Alliteration: Two or more words written close together which start with the same sound. Ed is described by Judy as a "patient person." This makes the phrase memorable. Think of all the alliterative names of characters you remember easily such as Mickey Mouse.

Chronology: Organisation of dates or events. In *Curious Incident* Siobhan reading extracts from Christopher's book makes us question the chronology. It is presented as a "play within a play."

Dramatic Irony: When the audience are aware of something that the characters are not. This creates dramatic tension. It could be argued that since many members of the audience would understand the communication of the characters better than Christopher, then much of the play contains dramatic irony. A more specific example would be when Christopher's father tells him his mother had to go to hospital when this wasn't the truth.

Ellipsis (plural Ellipses): Ellipses are used frequently by the playwright to show the characters thinking of which words to use and pausing as they do so. Ed's speech near the end of the play contains many ellipses to show him thinking about the words to get Christopher to trust him again. "And I… I have to show you that you can trust me… and it will be difficult at first because… because it's a difficult project."

Expletives: Swear words. They are used to show strength of feeling for example when Ed calls his son a "little shit."

Foreshadowing: An advance hint at something which will take place in the future. When Christopher first says to his father that he is planning on investigating the death of Wellington the dog his father reacts angrily, "You are to stop this ridiculous bloody detective game right now." His use of expletives and adjectives suggests that he might have had something to do with the mystery. We later learn that Ed did indeed kill the dog.

Metaphor: A comparison with something by stating that it is something else. The two things must be different, but contain a line of similarity. For example, "a pig of a day." Christopher doesn't like metaphors as he prefers everything to have its literal meaning.

Paradox: A combination of contradictory features. Christopher hates novels because they are fictional but here he is, a fictional character who has been writing a fictional novel whilst appearing in a fictional play!

Playwright: the person who wrote the play. Remember to refer to Simon Stephens in your answer (you can just use his surname but don't call him Simon!). Be careful to spell the term correctly, a common mistake is to write Playwrite…

Punctuation for effect: The use of punctuation that goes beyond its basic grammatical function and imbues meaning in a text. Seen, for example, through the playwright's numerous uses of ellipses.

Repetition: Deliberately repeating something which has already been written / said. Used to emphasise the importance of the repeated word or phrase. Seen when Christopher and Mrs. Shears are upset; near the end of the play, Ed requests a talk with Christopher his son initially repeats the word "No" seven times.

Sentence length: Variation of sentence length to create meaning. Short sentences within *Curious Incident* suggest a character struggling with the immediate situation. Ed, for example, is unable to form coherent sentences when he sees Christopher has found the letters from his mother, "These are. Oh shit. Oh Christ."

Simile: Like a metaphor a simile compares two things but generally using "as" or "like" in the phrase. A metaphor, in comparison, usually uses "is" or "was". Christopher has a dislike for metaphors but does occasionally use a simile such as, "The rain looks like white sparks."

Stage directions: Directions within a play that instruct actors on movement, expression, tone etc. Stephens does not use many stage directions in *Curious Incident* so those you find must be considered worthy of analysis. One memorable example would be, "Ed shakes Christopher hard… Christopher punches Ed repeatedly in the face."

Verb – a word which indicates an action. Verbs of note in *Curious Incident* include those denoting violence such as "thrashing," "punching," and "shaking."

CONCLUSION:

Studying a play such as *Curious Incident* allows us to examine how we as individuals approach difference… how understanding are you of others who might struggle to communicate as effectively as you? Are you patient and understanding or are you terse and snappy? Do you help and support those around you who might be having difficulties? There are some real issues about our changing abilities to communicate as we all become reliant on text messaging, social media and so on rather than honing our skills of non-verbal communication and conversation in "real" life.

Bibliography

The Guardian *"Through Innocent Eyes"*

https://www.theguardian.com/books/2004/apr/24/fiction.markhaddon

The Curious Incident of the Dog in the Night-Time and Detective Fiction

A Paper by Stefania Ciocia, Canterbury Christ Church University.

www.curiousonstage.com/education

nationaltheatre.org.uk/learning

The Curious Incident of the Dog in the Night-Time. An essay by Ted Gioia

www.postmodernmystery.com

Mark Haddon on *The Curious Incident of the Dog in the Night-Time* – Guardian book club

Printed in Great Britain
by Amazon